On the Day You Graduate

It's Time to Fly!

Carla M. Flanders

Illustrated by Annette Cable

Dedicated to my amazing husband and our sons who inspired, nurtured, and helped this book come to life.

Published by
CMF Marketing

Publisher's Cataloging-in-Publication Data
Carla M. Flanders.

On the day you graduate : it's time to fly! / Carla M. Flanders ;
Illustrated by Annette Cable. – Norton Shores, MI : CMF Marketing, 2025.

p. ; cm.

ISBN13: 978-0-9601299-0-4

1. Education. 2. Degrees, Academic 3. Children's books. I. Title. II. Cable, Annette.

LB14.7.F53 2025
370.1--dc23

Project coordination by Jenkins Group, Inc. | www.jenkinsgroupinc.com

Illustrations by Annette Cable

Design by Yvonne Fetig Roehler

Printed in the United States of America
29 28 27 26 25 • 5 4 3 2 1

A Keepsake for a Special Graduate

Use this page to record graduate's name, date, school, gift giver's name, special message, or anything else you would like to include.

Your arrival had been
anticipated for such a long time.

Preparations had been put into motion,
and excitement swirled around in the air.

On the day you came home,
hearts overflowed with joy!
Fears and worries dissipated,
and all eyes were on you.

Everyone wanted to be near you
and not let you out of their sight.

It was such a delight holding you,
rocking you, feeding you,
snuggling next to you,
and making sure you were safe and OK.

Before too long, it was time
for you to sleep in your crib.

We would check on you often, look at you
closely and watch while you peacefully slept.

As time went on, you started
moving and wiggling
around on your own.

For your safety,
we stood by your side;
we monitored you;
we held your hand.

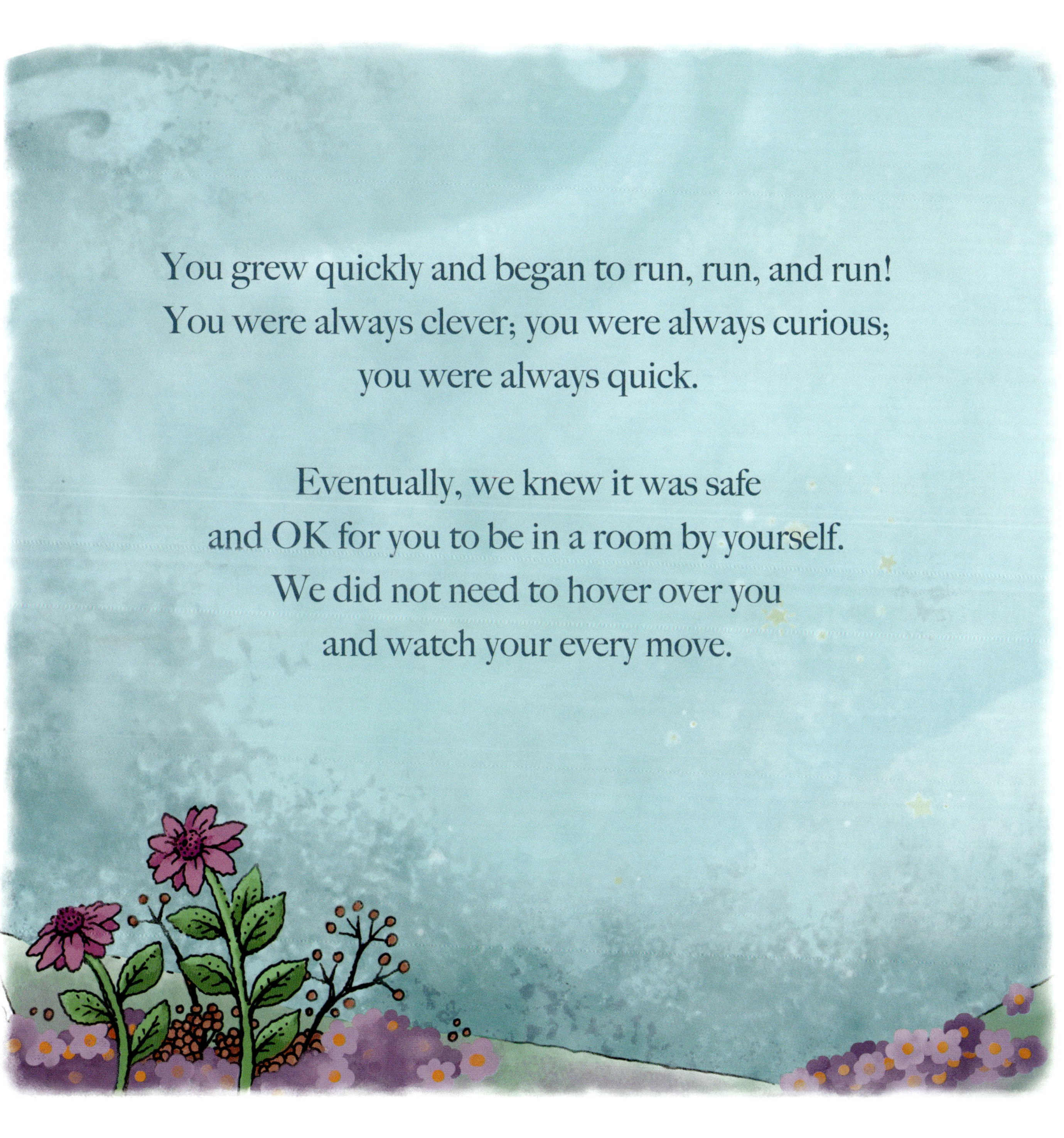
You grew quickly and began to run, run, and run!
You were always clever; you were always curious;
you were always quick.

Eventually, we knew it was safe
and OK for you to be in a room by yourself.
We did not need to hover over you
and watch your every move.

At nighttime, you loved books.

We would lie with you
for hours on end,
reading books, and
falling asleep by your side.

Before we knew it,
it was time for you to go off to school.

Time for you to be more independent,
explore, and learn.

Those first few days away were challenging
and so were many moments in the following years.

As you navigated through school, social activities,
family life, and beyond, there were many challenges.

Moments where you had to
figure things out on your own
because we were
no longer right by your side.

You managed them well
and came out stronger for it.

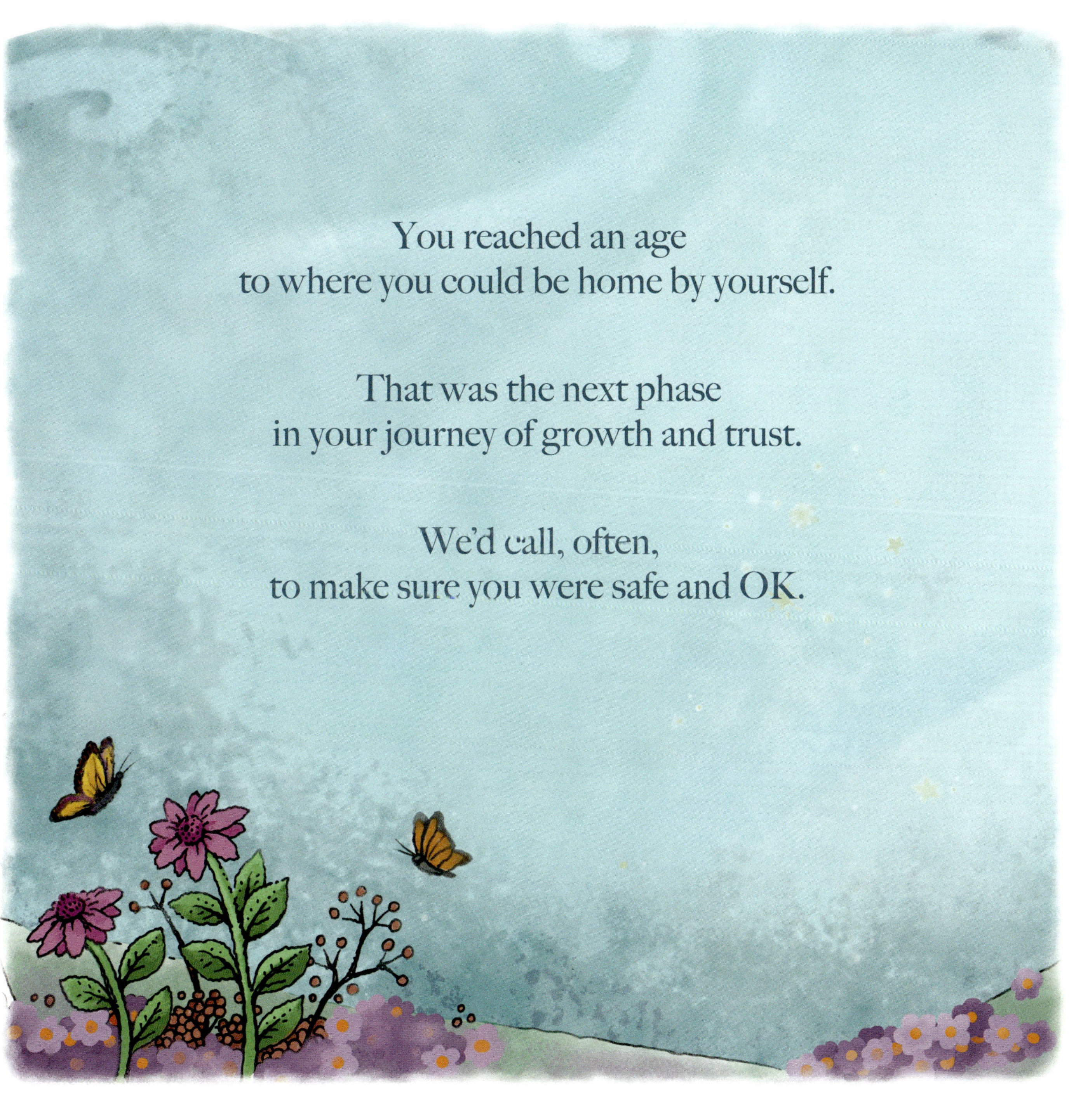

You reached an age
to where you could be home by yourself.

That was the next phase
in your journey of growth and trust.

We'd call, often,
to make sure you were safe and OK.

N
S
E
W

Then you received your driver's license
and were out on your own,
making your own choices,
making your own decisions,
and finding out more about yourself.

In a flash,
you were ready to
graduate!

It was time for you to spread your wings.

Time for you to leave our nest.

Time for you to explore the whole wide world
on your own. Time to fly!

Now, it is time to say goodbye to that little child
and say hello to the new adult
who is setting out to do extraordinary things!

We will always be here for you.
Whether we are by your side, in the next room,
down the road, or miles apart.

It's your time for discovery!

$E = mc^2$

It's your time to explore the person you are meant to be!
It's your time to shine!
We know you will do great things!

On the day you graduate, we honor who you were,
who you have become, and what you have learned.

CONGRAT

Now,

It's

We celebrate your achievements and your future aspirations.
We wish you everything you have ever hoped for,
and we take comfort in knowing you will be safe and OK.

Use these pages to record thoughts and ideas about . . .

What was your favorite memory from school?

Memories . . .

What subject did you enjoy most?

Who was your favorite teacher,
coach, or mentor and why?

What would you like to do after graduation?
Where do you see yourself in ten years?
Future
Dreams . . .
What will make your future self happy?
Summit

These pages are for others to share their memories or future dreams for you!
Reach for the Stars!

Ask a teacher to write you a note, set this book out at your graduation party, have friends sign their names, or nudge family members to provide words of wisdom and encouragement.

time to Fly!